# HOW TO TAKE OVER TEH WURLD

# HOW TO
## TEH

# AKE OVER
# WURLD

**A LOLcat
Guide 2 Winning**

**Professor Happycat
& icanhascheezburger.com**

GOTHAM
BOOKS

GOTHAM BOOKS
Published by Penguin Group (USA) Inc.
375 Hudson Street, New York, New York 10014, U.S.A.

Penguin Group (Canada), 90 Eglinton Avenue East, Suite 700, Toronto, Ontario M4P 2Y3, Canada (a division of Pearson Penguin Canada Inc.); Penguin Books Ltd, 80 Strand, London WC2R ORL, England; Penguin Ireland, 25 St Stephen's Green, Dublin 2, Ireland (a division of Penguin Books Ltd); Penguin Group (Australia), 250 Camberwell Road, Camberwell, Victoria 3124, Australia (a division of Pearson Australia Group Pty Ltd); Penguin Books India Pvt Ltd, 11 Community Centre, Panchsheel Park, New Delhi – 110 017, India; Penguin Group (NZ), 67 Apollo Drive, Rosedale, North Shore 0632, New Zealand (a division of Pearson New Zealand Ltd); Penguin Books (South Africa) (Pty) Ltd, 24 Sturdee Avenue, Rosebank, Johannesburg 2196, South Africa

Penguin Books Ltd, Registered Offices: 80 Strand, London WC2R ORL, England

Published by Gotham Books, a member of Penguin Group (USA) Inc.

First printing, September 2009
10  9  8  7  6  5  4  3  2  1

Gotham Books and the skyscraper logo are trademarks of Penguin Group (USA) Inc.

ISBN 978-1-592-40516-9

Printed in the United States of America
Set in IMPACT
Designed by Ben Gibson

While the author has made every effort to provide accurate telephone numbers and Internet addresses at the time of publication, neither the publisher nor the author assumes any responsibility for errors, or for changes that occur after publication.  Further, the publisher does not have any control over and does not assume any responsibility for author or third-party Web sites or their content.

We dedicashuns dis manual to all teh kittehs out dere strugglings under teh yoke of incompitent hoomin servidudes and duddetts.

# ACKNOLLIGE—
## AGNOWLEDGE—

**THX**

Professor Happycat nd hiz staff wud liek 2 thx all uv teh kittehs who contribyooted 2 dis vry important manual—dis buk wud nawt be possibel wifout u. <3 He wud awlso liek 2 thx teh 2 hoomins hoo so vry kindly offerd 2 proofreed da buk 4 us, tho I fink u will agree dat it wuz nawt nessesry.

And 2 all teh kittehs who didnt maek it: keep tryings an nevers gives up (speshully when ur hungree). Teh wurld wil be awrs soon 'nuff.

...but then the plan went horribly awry.

The skies
falling!
Must go
in NOW!!!

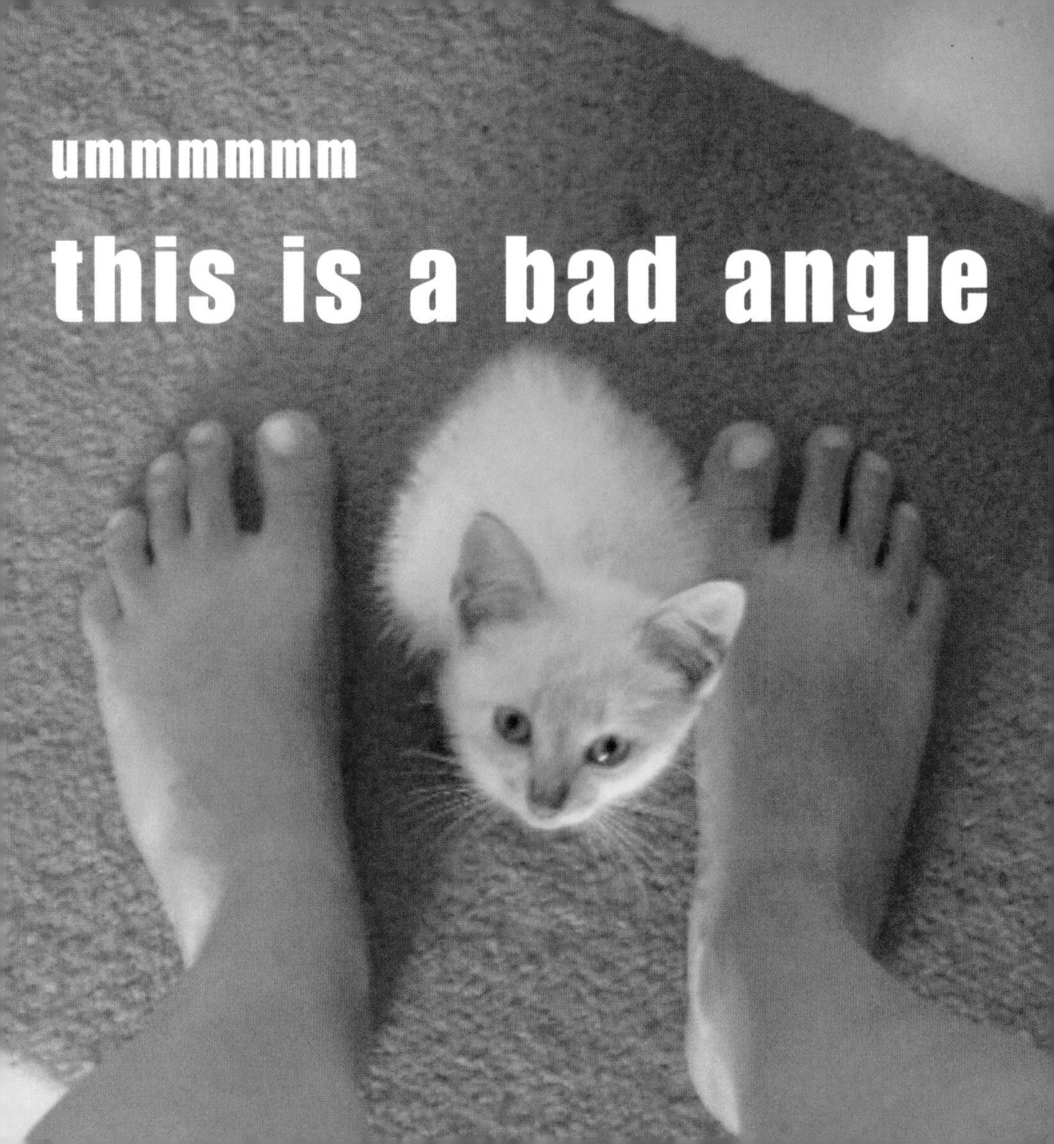
ummmmmm
this is a bad angle

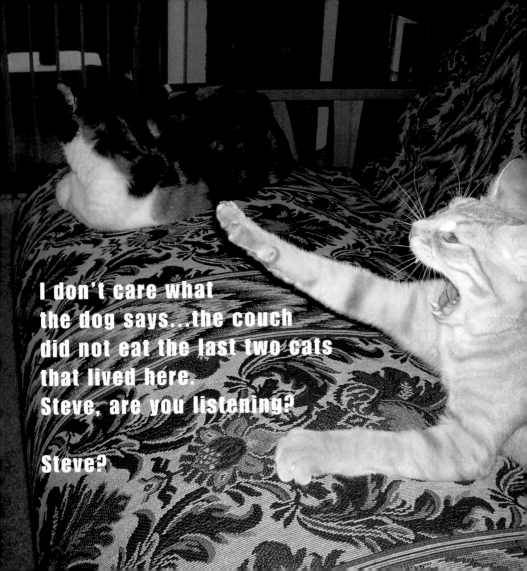

Silly hoomin. Duz u think
u can disstrackt us wif
beeds and bobbles??
Oooo
shinee

MONDAY ARE
$1.00 MARGARITA DAY
SEAFOOD • SALADS
da hoomanz r
slowlee lernin
lolspeak

'09 Kitteh Rezolushunz
Ai will nawt nom haus plantz and spend
teh nite hallucinating under ur bed.

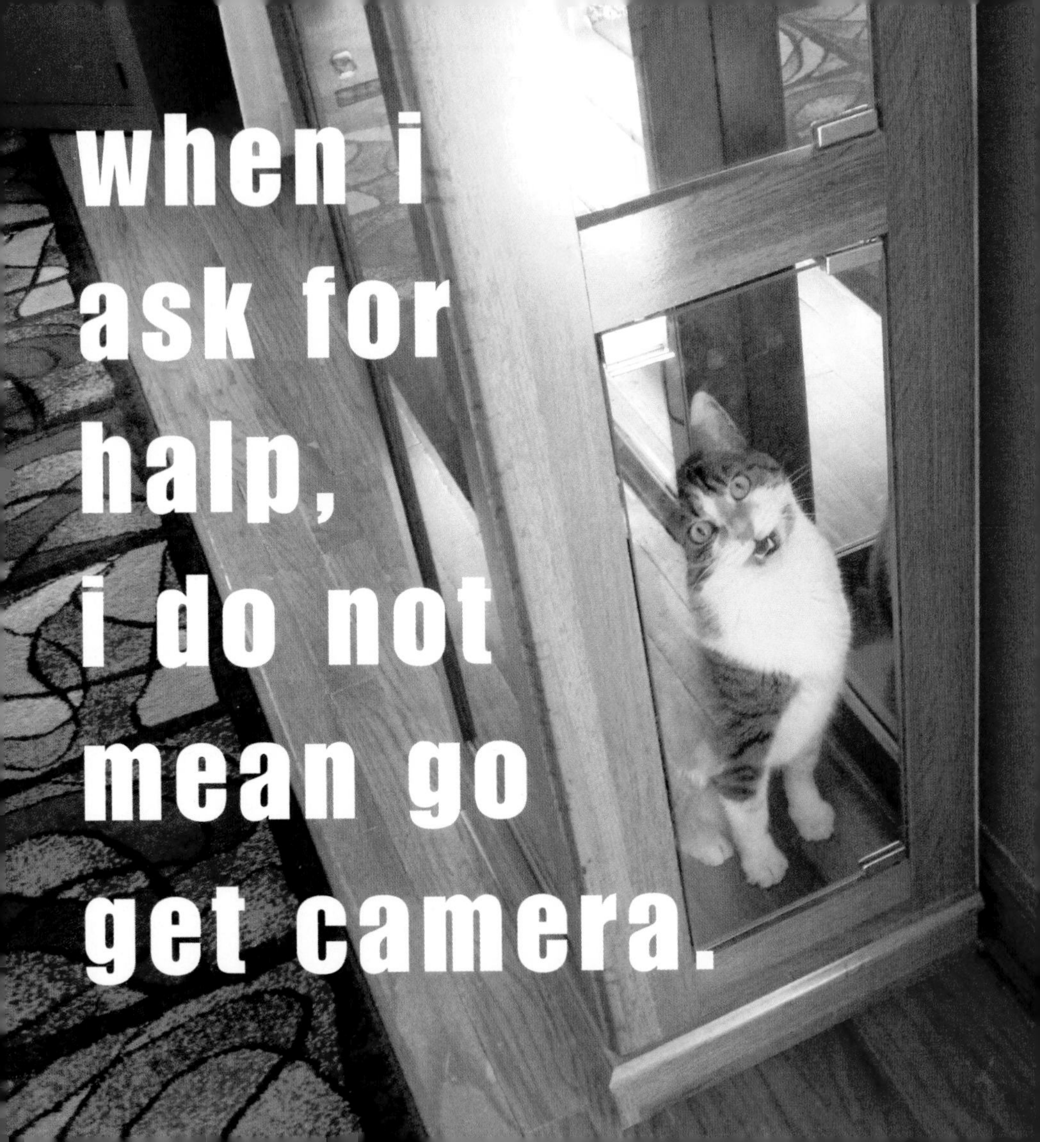
when i ask for halp, i do not mean go get camera.

# Nearsighted kitteh

has worked 4 minuts overtime...

again

carpit haz a flavr
simlr to mai but.

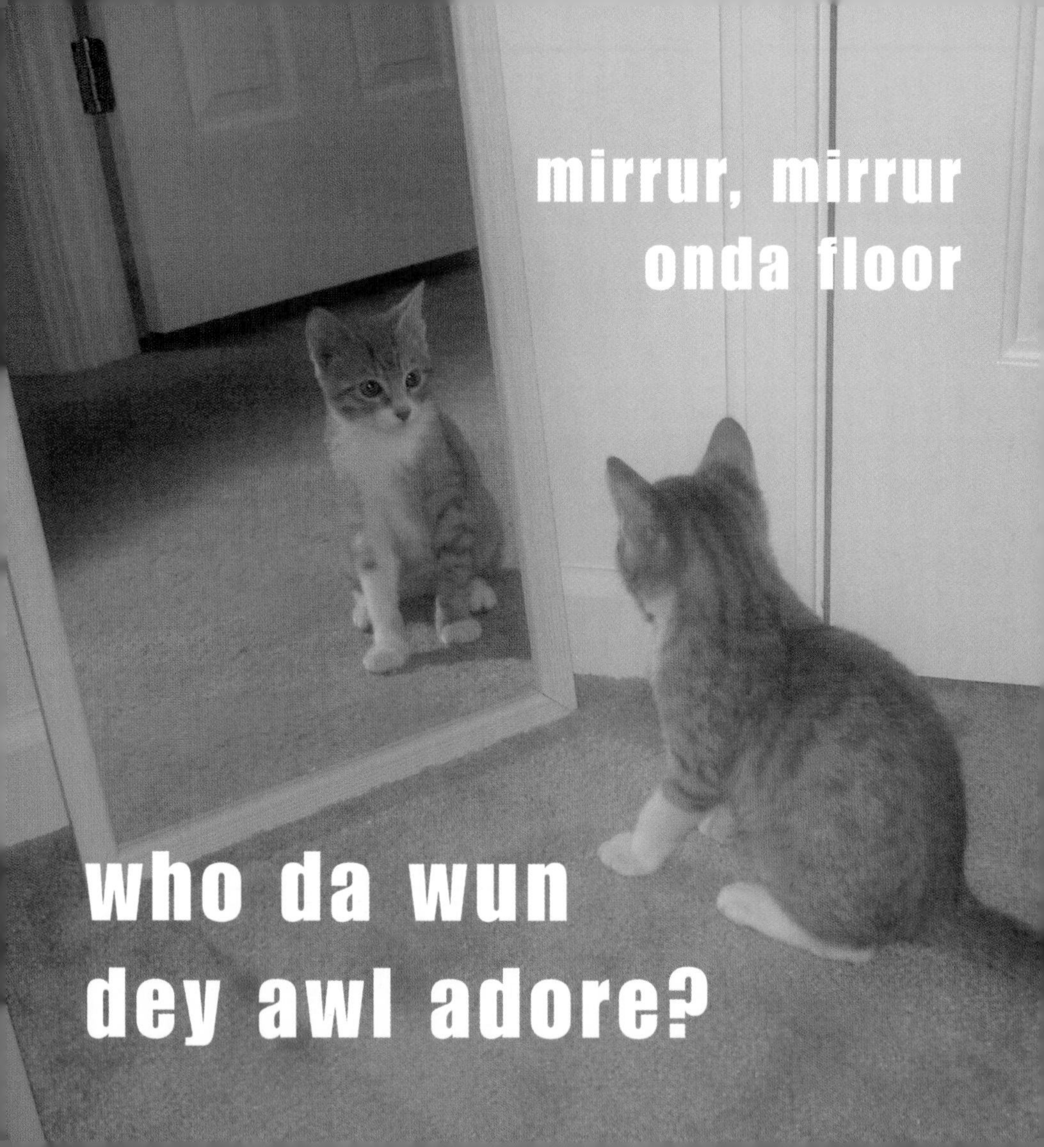
mirrur, mirrur
onda floor
who da wun
dey awl adore?

Mai pillow haz a flavr

nuther story...?

If u tink i noe
respek u in deh mornin
Den we jus sleeps til
deh afternoon

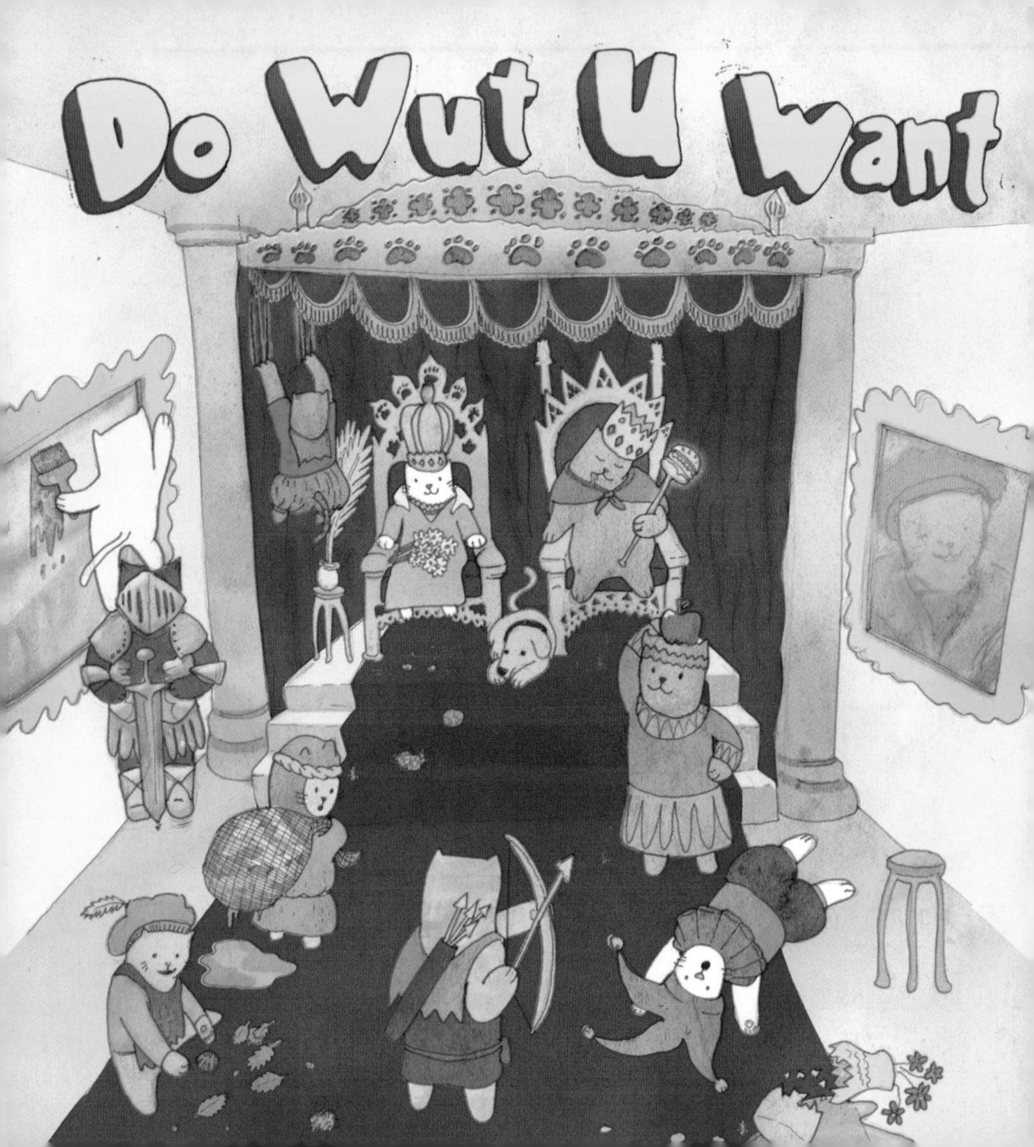
Do Wut U Want

It had taken months of sneaking into the laundry room at night, but Beanie now had one of every sock in the entire house.

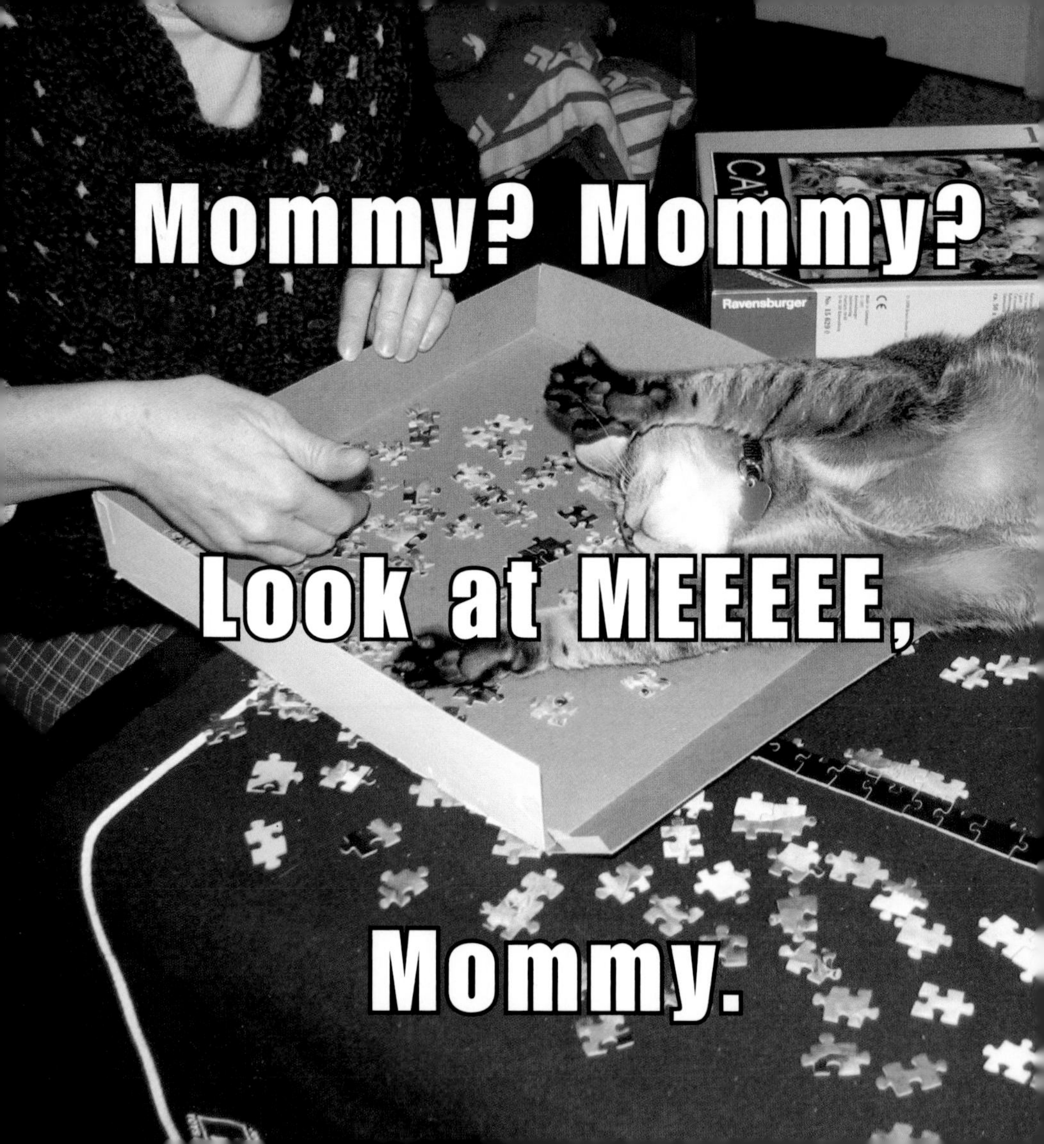
Mommy? Mommy?
Look at MEEEEE,
Mommy.

You know
I'm walking in that,
right?

Making a fur deposit
at the sweater bank

Dat nawt fud . . .

DAT wut fud eats.

U rly tink dat's enuff? Wat if zombies attack and u can't go to store? Den wat?

I waitz here for cheezburgers

O hai, waiter. Combo numbr 5 kthxbai.

That baby foods not taste nothing like baby.

Lead me
not into temptashun
Is can find it myself

food bowl...

ran out...

havent eaten...

in 5 min...

I haz can cheezburger

. . . and this is my Aunt Matilda who came over on the Mayflower

yeah, grate idea.
les play lolzilla
u beez Tokyo

One day I become shedding, bad-tempered butterfly.

I iz in ur bowl
bein ur froot

Kill Dem
Till They Die
Beware
Cats!
Hoomanz weaknizez
Kaynine weaknizez

I will wait

fishy cant hold

his breth 4ever

# DEATH

## wears a cute little bow

lazer cat spots his next victim

I has three years Excel and Powerpoint....

iz in no

mood

for yor

assback

IF YOU MUST INSISIT ON BATHTIME
THEN I MUST INSIST ON REENACTING PROHIBITION

Hint.

Ur in boks iz now
mai out boks...
...if u no what i meen

big hoomin
porselin
contrapshun...
... i will
lern your
seekrits
The Toilet Trained Cat
The Toilet Trained Cat
train your cat to use the human toilet
... and never scoop litter again
Aston Lau

curious kitteh ruins photo op

but I'z indoor kitteh
no wants go get sum fresh air

i luvs
new tummy rub fing

# The lesser-known "Schrödinger's Tube" experiment.

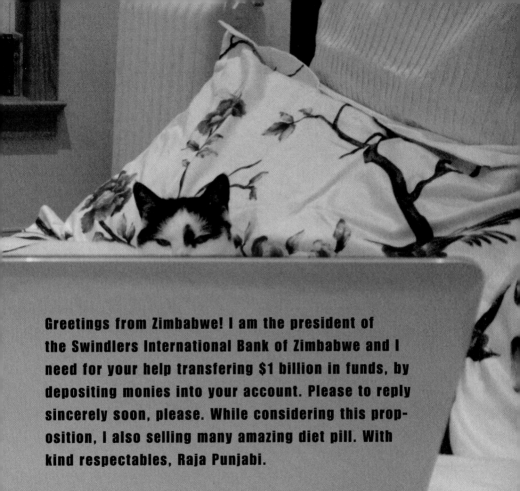

Greetings from Zimbabwe! I am the president of the Swindlers International Bank of Zimbabwe and I need for your help transfering $1 billion in funds, by depositing monies into your account. Please to reply sincerely soon, please. While considering this proposition, I also selling many amazing diet pill. With kind respectables, Raja Punjabi.

# K.

Box need
sum graond ruls.

why u get all difrent kindz liqers and iz only has 1 kindz foodz??

r dey gon?

**Leev alone
Iz havin duvet dai**

did we at leest come frum teh same store?

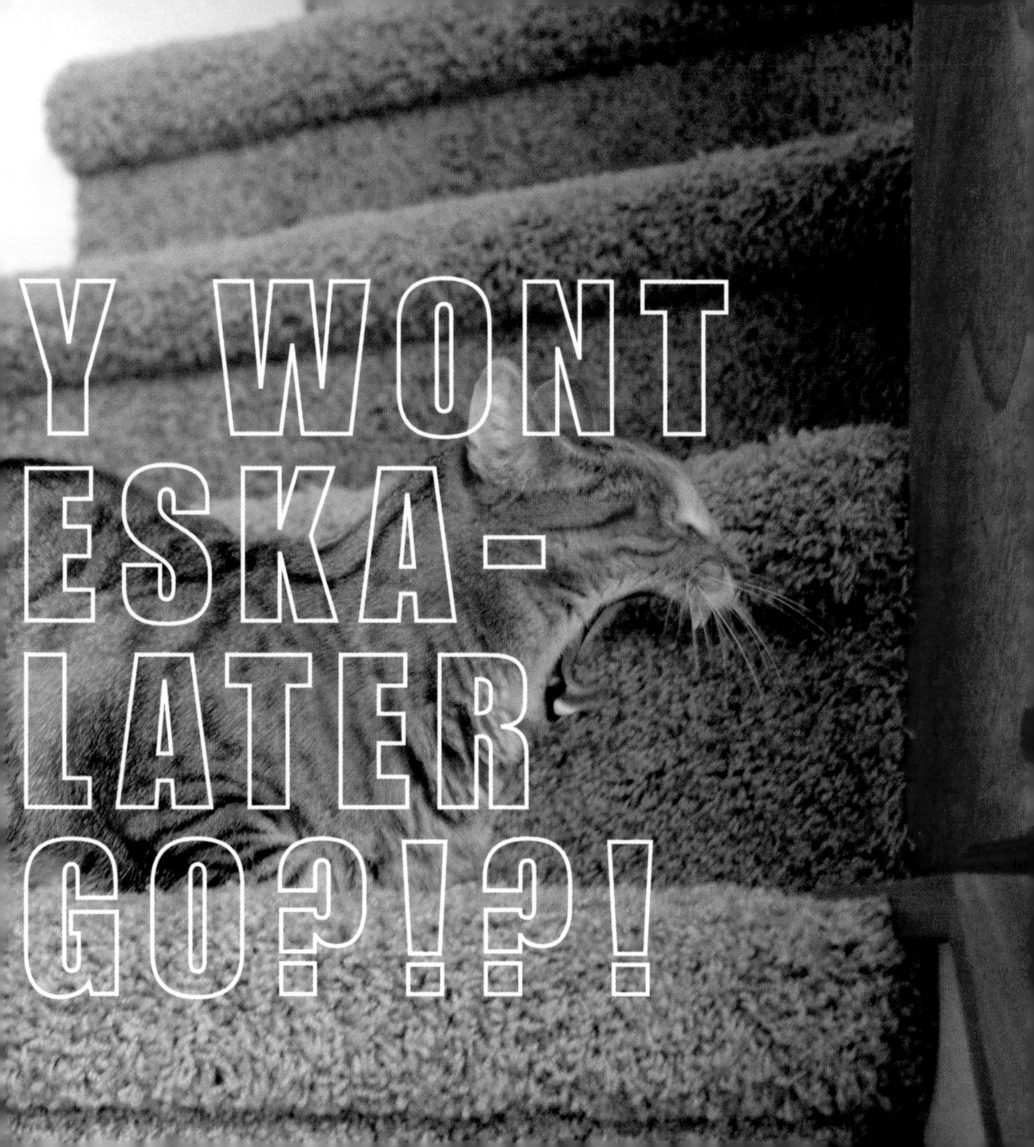
Y WONT
ESKA-
LATER
GO?!?!

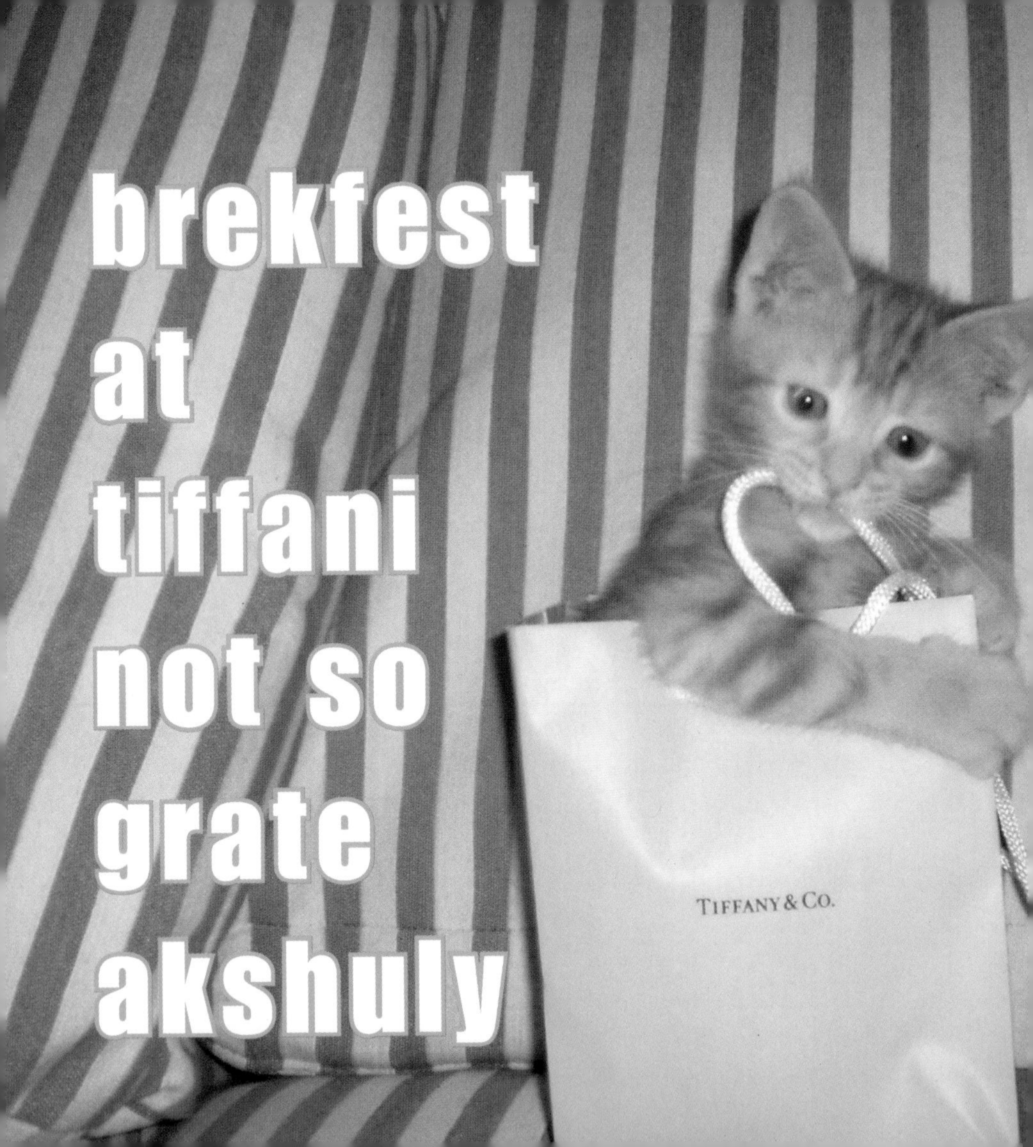
brekfest
at
tiffani
not so
grate
akshuly
TIFFANY & CO.

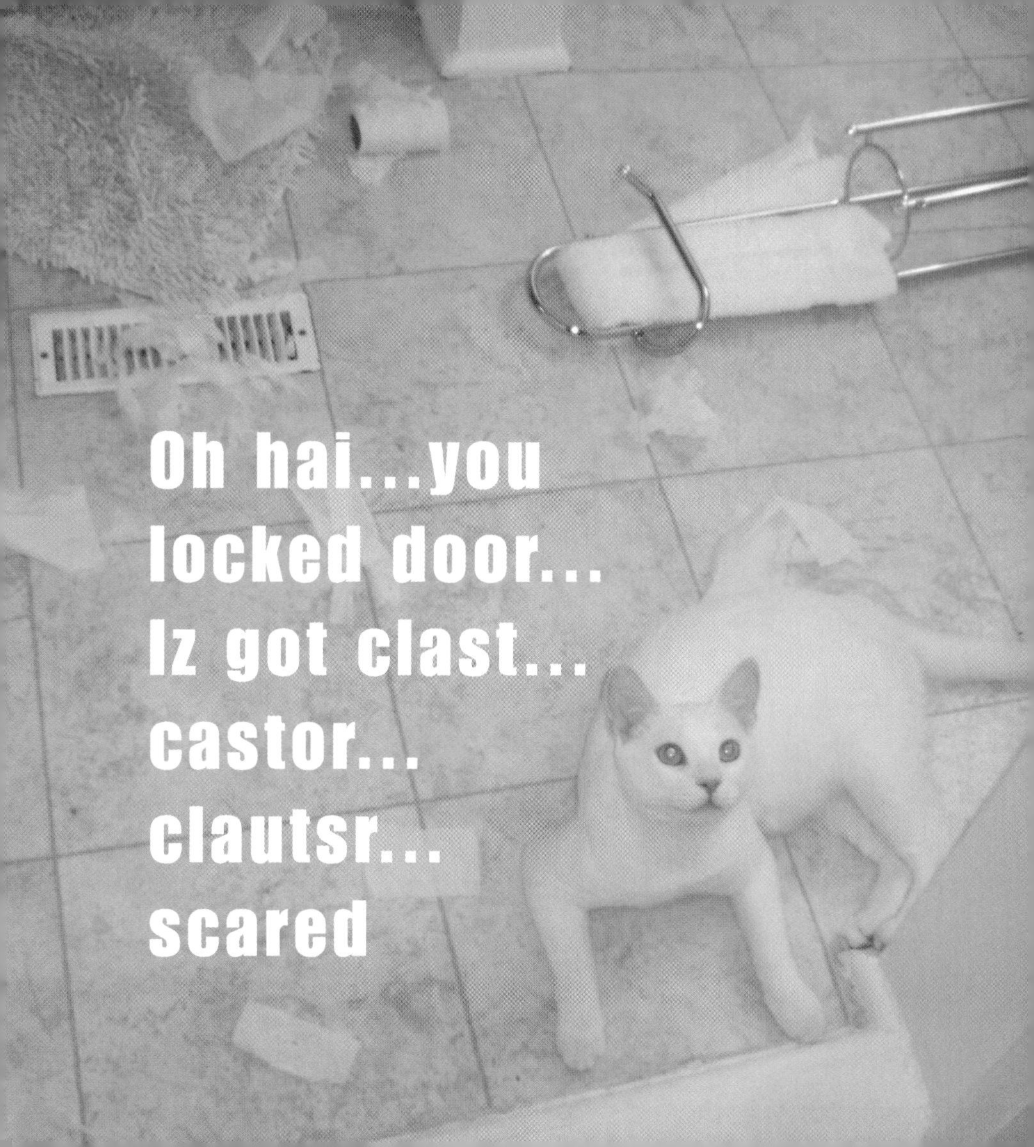
Oh hai...you
locked door...
Iz got clast...
castor...
clautsr...
scared

u has just changed
dats all

but but...
doesn't teh sand stik to ur fur?

Invisible Suction Cups

Mime
kitteh
looks
around
invisible
corner

Invisible Tarzan vine

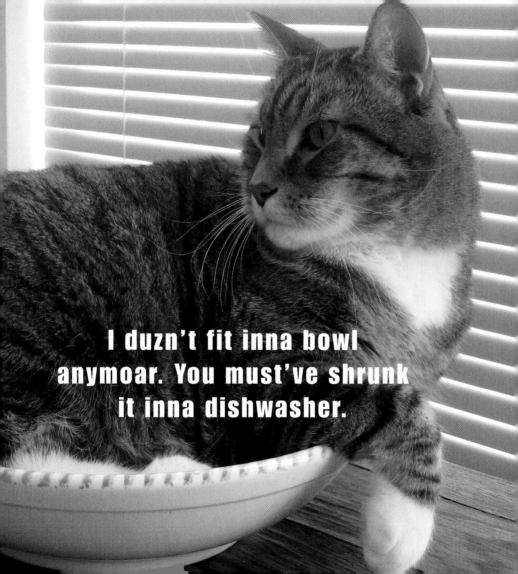

Iz hard to remembers any one particlar sanswhich

Windows

A fatal exception 0E has occurred at 0028:C0011E36 in VXD UMM(01) +
00010E36. The current application will be terminated.

*  Press any key to terminate the current application.
*  Press CTRL+ALT+DEL again to restart your computer. You will
   lose any unsaved information in all applications.

                Press any key to continue _

I cannot
confurm or
denai
I haz anyfing
to do wif dis

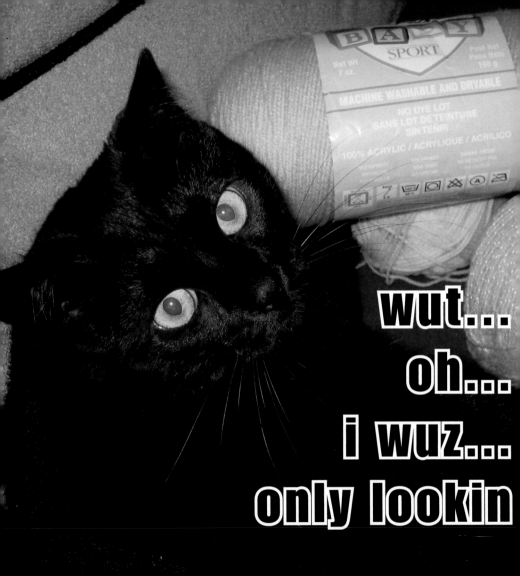

If anyone asks,
we were
together at
the mall.

**PRODUCTION CREDITS: Ben Huh: Editing & writing • Sonya Vatomsky: Editing • Joe Rufa: Illustrations • Kittehs: Lookin' good! IMAGE CREDITS, BY CHAPTER:**

## Bewar of menni danjurs

| LOLcat | Thx to |
|---|---|
| ...but then the plan went horribly awry. | Jackie & Bella Fraser |
| The skies falling! Must go in NOW!!! | Photography by Dee Conroy. For the love of her cat, Kramer, and her hubby Mike. |
| Leroy suspected a trap, but hey...c'mon...fuzzy chicken on a string! | Sarah Miller & Meghan James & Mr. Fred Poopers, Esq. |
| ummm this is a bad angle | Raíza, Maceió-al, Brazil |
| College kittehs Ecsperiment wit grass | Georgia (George), Carter, and Flori (Fuzzy) and their hoominz Joanna and Armando Nunez |
| no skwish! i be gud! | Joe Harrison / Pedra |
| I don't care what the dog says... the couch did not eat the last two cats that lived here. Steve, are you listening? Steve? | Kristen Bradford |
| Silly hoomin. Duz u think u can disstrackt us wif beeds and bobbles??Oooo shinee | Misty Cavit and Patrick Cavit. Kittens: Bacon (left) and Taters (right) |
| da hoomanz r slowlee lernin lolspeak | To Mom, Dad and Chopstick: DIS MY PAW! -- Love, Wonton |
| with horror, bongo realized that what happens at the vet's STAYS at the vet's | Sowisko, Zebe, Pluto & Fredek |
| '09 Kitteh Rezolushunz Ai will nawt nom haus plantz and spend teh nite hallucinating under ur bed. | Pokey Howell - from feral to superstar! |
| when i ask for halp, i do not mean go get camera. | Lisa & Jason Grimes -- In loving memory of Mavis "Mazie" Baker |
| Nearsighted kitteh has worked 4 minuts overtime...again | Martin R and Trance the cat, from Germany |
| dog lied....that big white bowl NOT jacuzzi | Paula Schuler and Xander |
| hot...lishious...hot...lishious...hot... horrible conundrums. | Wayne A. Chandler (and Giza!) |
| *sigh* u wunna start packing ur bags? ai awredi did, en yours oo.. | Alex Krall, Sara Ben-Abdallah, and Nicole DeMarco |
| Juz az I thawt! U benz byin teh cheep kitteh fudz! | Julia M. DeBlasio (ATLFosterMama), Fozzie the cat and http://www. atlantahumane.org/ |
| Plz don't send me away. I b gud honest..... | Amy Holloway at www.fforforum. co.uk |

## Bewar of menni danjurs

| LOLcat | Thx to |
|---|---|
| gremlin cat touched water | Nate & Rachel Coraor, Chris Gottschall |
| How could you do this to me? | Rebecca Scheiblauer |
| carpit haz a flavr simlr to mai but. | Mattea Cross at http://yexy. deviantart.com |
| scuse me but i believe was herez firzt | Dan Roden |
| deez eggs hav expired | Sarah Berkebile and Trinity |

## Charms to Disarm

| LOLcat | Thx to |
|---|---|
| yeh yeh rait der bit to da leftder! yesssssss | KamikazeKatze and Ferry the cat |
| dis one dedicates to da ladeez | Melanie Carnsew and L'il Buckaroo |
| who iz this handsome fellow? | Mariko Zervos |
| u has betraid my tiny trust | J² Holmes |
| mirrur, mirrur onda floorwho da wun dey awl adore? | Charlie by Stacey Bradbury |
| gold, frankensence,and purr | Tracey Carpenter & Adam Noce... and Pants the cat |
| wai ur hed juss expload?waz it mai cuteness? sry | Przemyslaw Zak |
| Mai pillowhaz a flavr | Cisca Steenkamp |
| Jus 5 more minitsPLEEEEEEZE?? | Sarah Chambers & Charlie Puss |
| You iz bluffing..right? | Sancho, Cliff & Olivia |
| I aksd mom not 2 part mah hair fer skool pitcher... luks stoopid. | Paula Hulick and Emma |
| Don't jus stand der!! Get meh 10cc of creem an 400 gms of toona gushy fuds!! STAT!!AN SUMBUDY PAGE DR. TINYCAT!!11!! | Michelle & Brian & the cats - Scotch, Merlin & Mia |
| nuther story...? | Terri Affanato-McAvoy and Tony |
| If u tink i noe respek u in deh morninDen we jus sleeps til deh afternoon | Jana, Callie & Indy Day |

## Do wut u want

| LOLcat | Thx to |
|---|---|
| Ebil plan, u sez? Sure, i haz some free tiemz. | Michele Banks & Teapot |
| We haz moddifyed ur blooprints tew meet r needz | Snickers and Salem (a.k.a. Basement Cat), Dan and Cynthia Jones |
| I accept ur toy gift... an will proseed to ignor it. | Mitsoo Svenke |

## Do wut u want

| LOLcat | Thx to |
| --- | --- |
| Yep, dis is definitivly teh BEST place | Amy Dunn & Tigger "Caboose" Dunn |
| I'm in yer weddin dress plottin yer divorce from Jerkface | Krystine Neuscheler and Little Dude |
| I know de is cleen U expect me to sleep on dirties? | Jamie Scott Picon and Daniel Walters. In memory to Kairo. |
| I don't know what that was, but you're gonna need a new one. | Leo by Cattails K. Kennedy |
| It had taken months of sneaking into the laundry room at night, but Beanie how had one of every sock in the entire house. | Fraidy Cat, Roly Poly, and Mitchie Witch |
| da drawer wuz in da way of my comfurt so i moved it | Crystal, Jeffrey and Marcus Teissedre (aka The 2 Ceders) |
| Mommy? Mommy? Look at MEEEEE, Mommy. | Ian Pol helps Mama Bec with a puzzle—photo by Joanne "Carpwoman" Pleskovich |
| Iz maks you sum origamees No thx me now...later OK | Gene Dershewitz and Bootsie |
| cuddling! sure beats doin' stuff. | Saechalyn |
| drunk dial kitteh is callin u at 2am | Saren ni'Haeghan and Sebby |
| You know I'm walking in that, right? | Dave Orloski, Cindy Lou, Miss Puggy, Jack & Liz |
| Psst...Wanna buy sum nip? | Daniel Neal & Goblin Neal |

## Eat ur fud. And ebbryone elses too.

| LOLcat | Thx to |
| --- | --- |
| Dat nawt fud...Dat what fud eats. | Gigi the kitten by Beverly Dawn Hembree |
| U rly tink dat's enuff? Wat if zombies attack and u can't go to store? Den wat? | Kerry Knight and Baby |
| wut u meen iz nat fud?Iz in a bowl! | Lisa R Ottenberg |
| i TOLD u i wuz so hungreei cud eet a hors | Cally Swanson |
| really funny, guysnow where is it | Monty & joeface034 (www.spinandcynicism.com) |
| Cheezburger deposit box | Ausenda Mangerona and Kelly the cat |
| u can haz my leftoverz i picked out all teh shrimps...sry | Janet Daly |
| i waitz here for cheezburgers | Judy Council and Peep Brown |
| O hai, waiter. Combo numbr 5 kthxbai. | "Fats" -- photo by Karen Jessee, submitted by Danny Jessee |
| If perchance you're tired of eatin' it I could eat it. | Heather Hammer & Sam the cat |
| A really fancee feest wud hav candles. 'm jus sayin'. | Malachite Dragon & Cassandra (aka BabyGirl) |
| That baby foods not taste nothing like baby. | Dawn Sartz & Baby at www.scottishcat.com |

## Eat ur fud. And ebbryone elses too.

| LOLcat | Thx to |
| --- | --- |
| Why it saiz Turkey? It no haz flavor... | Jackie & Bella Fraser |
| Lead me not into temptashun Is can find it myself | Photo by Madison Davis |
| food bowl....ran out... havent eaten... in 5 min... | Rosie Catalano, Bryony & Teddy "bin face" Heath |
| I haz can cheezburger | Chris Evans |

## Inpers- imparsen- copycat

| LOLcat | Thx to |
| --- | --- |
| Marie Catoinette accepts her fate | Christina D Jones |
| yeah, grate idea. les play lolzilla. | Kristin & Edgar "fuzzy-britches" Morris |
| u beez Tokyo | |
| let them eat caek! | Katie Dodd, Delilah and 'Dinger |
| Japan has Godzilla. Bethlehem has Floyd. | happilykim.wordpress.com |
| Bellhop Kitteh will take your bags now. | Lisa, Scott and Twinkie (The Orange Assassin) Marshall |
| Copy Cat | Melissa J Pearce |
| Life imitates art. Or is it the other way around? | Frank, Carol, Cari and Nacho Jarchow |
| Black hole cat stealin ur gravity | Errol from www.welovealpacas.co.nz |
| One day I become shedding, bad-tempered butterfly. | Elliott Beard and Sergeant Squirmy |
| potion iz warn off! i cat agen | Katherine, Eleanor, Heidi |
| I iz in yr bowl bein ur froot | Hizome |

## Kill dem till they die frum it

| LOLcat | Thx to |
| --- | --- |
| I will wait. fishy cant hold his breth 4ever | Raz Rasmussen and Fiona, Carly Lu's Flight Blog (http://likambo.com/flyblog) |
| If you don't like my changes I can always edit your face | "Aggie the Educated Cat" by Sally McNeilley |
| GREAT. now i killedz her... who gonna feedz meh?? | Amber and Piña |
| For a present, < Pull here. | InCatNation + The Big Gornowski |
| DEATH Wears a cute little bow | Judy Letostak |
| Threat eliminated. | Greg and Mary Jo Hendrickson & Roxie (the cat) |
| lazer cat spots his next victim | Johnna Lee Tait |

## Know ur skillz

| LOLcat | Thx to |
| --- | --- |
| I has three years Excel and Powerpoint......and excellent cuddle skillz | Sandy Johnson and Buster |

## Know ur skillz

| LOLcat | Thx to |
| --- | --- |
| snail kitteh stalks u...very slowly | 001.jpg - Kadri Elcoat & Patches the Itteh Bitteh Kitteh from Sunflower Lodge |
| Determination. | Bert Plat |
| wurld dominashun—planning phase | Sarah McElhinney |
| dis game wud be so much easier if we werent color blind | Kristen Quigley and Kyle Wilson |
| Finished yer taxes...U may want to sit down.. | Michelle Thaller and Keiki |
| ellavayter butt in 3.....2.....1 | Valerie Heimerich and Dr. Simon, F.M.A. |
| Da doc said ta spend 30 minutes using da weights. I can do that. | Dawne Howes, with help from Brady, Gisele, Bandit, Potato and Pun. Tanks to da Pat Brody Shelter for Cats & Priscilla Deschamps, and to Heather Gainer for getting me addicted to IcanHasCheezburger.com. |
| I cannot brain today I have the dumb | In honor of Ballou Banks, who brings joy to his owners, Kristin and Diane Banks |

## Lay down da law

| LOLcat | Thx to |
| --- | --- |
| I shall name this place...Catadonia! | Shannon Durval & Bella |
| first U mus answer meh riddles three. if U are rite, den U may pee! | "Cheesecake" by Sally McNeilley |
| iz in no mood for yor sassback | Beedie, who unwillingly allowed Erik and Sonya Luchauer to take his picture. |
| Put it back where u found it. We dun need anymore petz around here. | Bradmo the photographer, Amelia the skin kitten, and Arisu the cat. |
| See dis chart, hooman? It show mayjer decreases in my nom and snooze numberz...I wood like to hear how u planz to korrect dis. | Kip & Kody |
| IF YOU MUST INSISIT ON BATHTIME THEN I MUST INSIST ON REENACTING PROHIBITION | |
| Alienz called mah dish They wants tuna | Jennifer Cote as dictated by Neechee |
| I divided the room. Left side's mine. So's the right. | Mary Lou Willits and Max |
| Suitcase kitteh sez iVacashun denied.i | Julia C Mundy and Mara the Firecat |
| and if you continue to bathe me in the sink i will scratch you here, here, here, here and here | Amelia C Pantalos and Peter |

## Lay down da law

| LOLcat | Thx to |
| --- | --- |
| I iz waiting fur teh fishies. Stoopid humin! Get to work. | Catherine Mader |
| i'z gonna sleep here u can has my bed | Winston Brodkin and Family |
| And do U Know Y i Has called U in here? | The Big Cat |
| I can has snuggles? No. | Janicia, Thierry and Thumper - (janicia.blogspot.com) |
| wut u doin heer wifout ma mai tai? bak u go. an huree up, iz firsty. | Steffen Wittig |
| Hint. | Ashlee Elledge |

## Lurn noo technologies

| LOLcat | Thx to |
| --- | --- |
| Ur in boks iz now mai out boks...... if u no what i meen | "Wooster" by Christian J Simpson www.superhighstreet.com |
| big hoomin porselin contrapshun...... i will lern your seekrits | Aston and Miki of ToiletTrainedCat.com |
| curious kitteh ruins photo op | Christopher B. Romeo |
| but I'z indoor kitteh no wants go get sum fresh air | Stacey Hala (Hamner) and Zephyr |
| No wonder dems hoomins write funny. Dis be hard. | Kate |
| We wuz told computah had mice | In memory of our precious "Granite": the sweetest rescue cat the world may ever know. May heaven be filled with snuggles and sparkly bits. We will love you always. |
| RETINAL SCAN COMPLETE Acess Granted. Welcome back Agent Meow | Vitara & muriell, P.A.W. In loving memory of Saffron. |
| i luvs new tummy rub fing | Jill Sanchez and Kitty |
| The lesser-known iSchrödinger's Tube experiment. | Schnoodle and Sammy |
| Greetings from Zimbabwe! I am the president of the Swindlers International Bank of Zimbabwe and I need for your help transfering $1 billion in funds, by depositing monies into your account. Please to reply sincerely soon, please. While considering this proposition, I also selling many amazing diet pill. With kind repectables, Raja Punjabi. | The Marchitto Family |

## Make allies... or nawt

| LOLcat | Thx to |
| --- | --- |
| Is there space for meh nao? How about nao? What about nao? Nao? No No No No | Marcus Pierce & Laurie Taylor |
| I gotta move. Upstares naybor 2 annoying. | Justin Elam: Though absent you are always near, still loved, still missed and always dear |
| Tuff decishun for kitteh...choclat or vanila | Maggie Grindler, Tiger Lily, Dr. Chocolate, Mr. Cinnamon, and special thanks to Mama Buck. |
| K. Box need sum graond ruls. | Tarryn, Dion, Pudding & Fatboy |
| couples counseling: not going so well | Kristin Burniston |
| solvd ur fishtank problem. no needz wurry abowt furgeting to feedz fishus annymoar. iz alwaes plzd to halp u. | Camilla Lie & Muffin |
| akshully, that dress do makes ur butt look kinda big | Papaya by Paul Katcher |
| don worry I luvs u no mater ur color | Brenda Weaver, Beany and Little Bear |
| dis not wat i meen when said want sister | Melanie & Kevin & Parker |
| U see? U see how he tawntz meh? An dis iz when you iz home U shood see wat he do wen u nawt here...day after day after day... | Photo credit: Cristina Ungstad Yu. Model: Twitch McLaughlin Yu with unnamed squirrel. Website: braincandy408.wordpress.com |

## Master ur emoshuns

| LOLcat | Thx to |
| --- | --- |
| Bored cat is bored. | Liesl McQuillan |
| why u get all difrent kindz liqers and iz only has 1 kindz foodz?? | Ian and Amanda Scott with Esme |
| r dey gon? | Yatesh Singh |
| Nuthing canz stop our lub | Candido Resendez and Monty Cat |
| Tempur tantrumz Ai haz dem | Laura Hosbach and Toby cat |
| Teh media portrays unrialistik body-image ideels for teh young felines of today | Sammie 323 and Bubbie |
| Will someone PLEASE bring me the remote?! | Chloe by Marie Sweeten |
| Leev alone iz havin duvet dai | Angie Davidson, Sophie and www.sophiecat.co.uk |
| did we at leest come frum teh same store? | Evilqueen112 |
| I'm not talking to you I'm not talking to you either | Jaime Navetta, with special love to Indiana, Mona, Jake, HQ & Peen |

## Master ur emoshuns

| LOLcat | Thx to |
| --- | --- |
| u sed there would b cupcakes. u lied. | Lisa Cook |
| Y WONT ESKALATER GO?!?! | Lockshot (hoomin) and Bonzie (kitteh) |
| Oh no!kissin scene!! | Maria and Thomas |
| I hate mondays | Aimee Reed (Hoomin) + Hannah Reed (Kitteh) |
| lets pretend im sorry... and i feel rly bad...okai? | Olivia's Layla by Kirsten |
| i waz so totaly not surprized | Furgy - owner of Jenna Brown and Päivi Parkkinen |
| brekfest at tiffani not so grate akshuly | Aaron, Jenny, Bunker, Roxy, Munson & Abby Tillinger |
| Oh hai... you locked door...iz got clast...castor...clautsr...scared | Wendy James & Farnham |
| I play well with others......others, not you. | Cara Kimura - Cookie's hoomin |
| u has just changed dats all | Nacho Man and Pretty Girl rescued from Crash's Landing by the Kittels |
| but but...doesn't teh sand stik to ur fur? | Esther Cheng |
| Rezentment: I haz it. | Larkin Willis, Itty Bitty and Big Red |

## See wut udders can't see

| LOLcat | Thx to |
| --- | --- |
| INVISIBLE SYMPATHY | Mimi K Mead (photographer & Mom) & Kevin A Holbert (photo submitter & son). Socks (the skinny one) & Tigger (the chubby one) are 16 year old sisters who live with two other cats, Chloe (AKA "Stripey-pants") who's 15 yrs old & "P" our 14 year old gray male, and a crazy, wingnut dog, Tucker, who's 4 years old. We all miss our Blue Cream Point Himmie, Savannah, who we lost in October '08. This submission is dedicated to her. <3 |
| godzilla cat stomps invisible tokyo | Manuel Kaelin and his cat Lama |
| Invisible Suction Cups | Lennert Knoop, Veronika Cheplygina and Buffy; Delft, The Netherlands |
| Invisible broom. | Photographer: Natalie Scarpelli. Model: Echo von Monster. Web: flickr.com/byasphyxia |
| invisibul seesaw | Savannah Carlson and Sammy Pants |

## See wut udders can't see

| LOLcat | Thx to |
|---|---|
| Mime kitteh looks around invisible corner | Ryan and Amy DeCook and their kitteh Gordon |
| Invisible Tarzan vine | Sarah Morgan lives in Chicago with her two black and white short-hair cats, Haydn and Etienne, who will be two years old in May. When not sleeping, they love playing catch with plastic rings and people-watching from the apartment window. |

## Survive pointy fingers: deny, deny, deny

| LOLcat | Thx to |
|---|---|
| I duzn't fit inna bowl anymoar. You must've shrunk it inna dishwasher. | Gillian, Ryan and Gladiator |
| Dog did it<br>Duz we has a dog? | Carol Durand - Toby |
| New kitteh? Black u sez?<br>Nope, nawt seen. | Tammy, Evan, Misa and Bit |
| Teh dog?<br>hazznt seen it 4 sum tiem | Miezekatze by Bernhard Schriefer |
| weird, huh?<br>couch wuz just lik dis when I gets home too | Photo: Gatinha, neck massager and bug hunter extraordinaire. Taken by Danielle and Alexandre, Gatinha's proud parents in Brazil. |
| Iz hard to remembers any one particlar sanswhich | Photo by Rommel & Marie Marquez with special help from our cats Lulu and Wakka. |
| I cannot confurm or denai<br>I haz anyfing to do wif dis | Maz, Kai & Smoosh Pays |
| wot mayks u fink iz been nywer neer yr jewlry boks? | Angie Davidson, Sophie and www.sophiecat.co.uk |
| Honest!<br>We'll be good till you get home... now go! | Mama Kim and Papa Jon are proud of their furry children Jillybean and Georgio and would like to make a special dedication to the newest (non-furry) member of the family - Lillian Marie!! |
| wut...oh...<br>i wuz...only lookin | Booger and Natalie |
| If anyone asks, we were together at the mall. | Kittehs from Kamisha Exotics / "Bunzilla" complements of "Feline Inquisition" at Etsy |
| Don't look at me I didn't kill him | Andy Myers |
| Uh, da burdies gone to da moveez<br>Ai keepingz howz warmz for demz | Henry Rupert Hornby (HRH) loved, worshipped and adored by Noeleen and Alison |